BY BEV AISBETT

Living IT Up

Letting IT Go

Get Real

Taming the Black Dog

The Little Book of IT

Fixing IT

Recovery: A Journey to Healing

The Book of IT

Get Over IT

I Love Me

All of IT: A Memoir

Living with IT

30 Days 30 Ways to Overcome Anxiety

LIVING WITH IT

BEV AISBETT

HarperCollins*Publishers*

HarperCollins_Publishers_

First published in Australia in 1993
This edition published in 2019
by HarperCollins_Publishers_ Australia Pty Limited
ABN 36 009 913 517
harpercollins.com.au

HarperCollins_Publishers_
Level 13, 201 Elizabeth Street, Sydney, NSW 2000, Australia
Unit D1, 63 Apollo Drive, Rosedale, Auckland 0632, New Zealand
A 53, Sector 57, Noida, UP, India
1 London Bridge Street, London, SE1 9GF, United Kingdom
Bay Adelaide Centre, East Tower, 22 Adelaide Street West, 41st Floor, Toronto,
    Ontario, M5H 4E3, Canada
195 Broadway, New York, NY 10007, USA

National Library of Australia Cataloguing-in-Publication data:

Aisbett, Bev.
Living with it: a survivor's guide to panic attacks.
ISBN 978 1 46075 717 8 (paperback)
ISBN 978 1 74309 750 2 (ebook)
1. Panic attacks – Popular works. I. Title.
616.85223

Cover design by Hazel Lam, HarperCollins Design Studio
Cover illustration by Bev Aisbett
Printed and bound in Australia by McPherson's Printing Group
The papers used by HarperCollins in the manufacture of this book are a natural,
recyclable product made from wood grown in sustainable plantation forests.
The fibre source and manufacturing processes meet recognised international
environmental standards, and carry certification.

INTRODUCTION

I first encountered my **IT** on a glorious blue day in Sydney, on what was meant to be a pleasant weekend visit to attend the Australian National Cartoonists' awards — the 'Stanleys'.

The sky was a flawless canopy, the yachts bobbed cheerily on the harbour, tourists snapped photos of smiling friends on the foreshore, and there I stood, struck dumb by the enormity of what I was experiencing.

Most people who suffer Panic Syndrome (and suffer is the word!) remember their first Panic Attack.

It is overwhelming, utterly terrifying and remains etched on the memory for a long time afterwards.

Hence, a pattern develops, as this book shows.

In the months that followed this initial attack, I was to return again and again to sources of reassurance, support and understanding that would eventually steer me out of the troubled, turbulent waters of this condition and back into the real world.

In doing so, and in line with my chosen profession, I decided to create a handbook that would provide a ready guide, in a *patient's* language, to those same sources of help that saw me through this debilitating ailment.

As a survivor, I now pass on to fellow sufferers the kind of information and practices that were of great assistance to me, and in a form that will, hopefully, convey this information quickly, simply and with gentle disarmament, i.e. the cartoon.

My message to all Panic People is this: I *know* how you feel, and you *will* be well again. This book is testimony to that.

To those of you who may believe that your **IT** is far more fearsome than mine: while this is no competition (and if it were, what a useless one!), let me assure you that my **IT** woke me every day to the same tears and tremors and terrors that you may be feeling right now.

My thanks is beyond measure to all those who stood by me and, in particular, to one stranger who, without question or dismay, came to the aid of this bewildered soul on an unfamiliar street one dark, dark night, so long ago.

To all of you, take heart. One day this will be a far-off memory.

Trust me.

Trust yourself.

Bev Aisbett

CONTENTS

If you have picked up this book,
then you are probably experiencing
some very strange and frightening things ...

DOES THIS LOOK FAMILIAR?

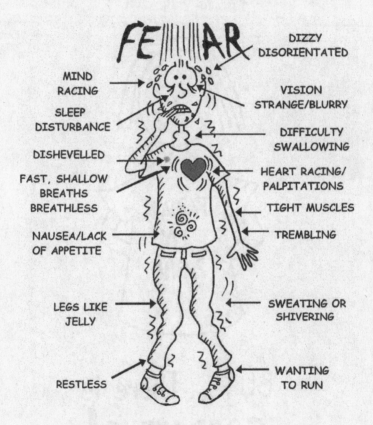

and overall, feelings of FEAR and DREAD that seem to come from NOWHERE?

Well, you have just joined **1000s** of people who have **PANIC ATTACKS***.

* also known as Panic Syndrome/Disorder, or Anxiety Syndrome/Disorder

BUT... There is
GOOD NEWS!

GOOD NEWS SECTION

YOU ARE NOT ALONE

At least 5% of the population has experienced Panic Attacks and there may be many more people who, for various reasons, keep their panic hidden. Others may not experience actual panic, but suffer very high levels of anxiety and unease.

And ... EVERYONE experiences anxiety at some stage in life! Yours is just turned up several notches!

YOU ARE NOT DYING

Though it may seem that way at times, these are only FEELINGS and IDEAS. Both will pass. Some people mistake  a Panic Attack for a heart attack or think that their heart cannot take the strain, but the heart is a tough muscle. It can cope. After all, this is only TEMPORARY.

YOU ARE NOT GOING MAD

What you are experiencing is a combination of FEARFUL THOUGHTS and PHYSICAL SENSATIONS, arising as a natural consequence of long-term unresolved STRESS.

Let's face it — you have NEVER handled stress very well, have you?

AND — THE BEST NEWS OF ALL ...

You **can** beat this!
You **will** get better!

PANIC STATIONS

It seems that out of a clear blue sky ...

... you are suddenly struck by the most overwhelming sense of TERROR and DREAD imaginable.

Your first instinct is to RUN, to flee from this agonising fear.

You go into full PANIC MODE — your heart races, you feel faint, you shake, you sweat ...

You can't imagine what could make you feel this terrible, so you search for a CAUSE ...

You decide you MUST be dying ...

... or going CRAZY ...

... or that you will FAINT!

Eventually, when these sensations subside and you find that nothing awful has happened to you, you breathe a sigh of RELIEF.

You have had your first PANIC ATTACK.

You have met **IT**.

The trouble is, your brain is now on the lookout for **IT**.

Since you're still alive, didn't faint and seem to be sane, what could **IT** be?

Because you don't know what **IT** is, or where **IT** came from, you figure **IT** could sneak up on you again at ANY time,

and **IT** was so HORRIBLE, you start to really worry ...

You spend a lot of time wondering if or when **IT** will strike again. You get SCARED. You get TENSE.

You become acutely aware of the slightest physical changes, and your mind EXAGGERATES them, believing they signal the return of **IT**.

Your mind is on RED ALERT. Your thoughts are racing. It's like you are tuned into ten different radio stations in your head.

By morning you are EDGY and IRRITABLE ...

... which makes you feel ...

MEA CULPA

GUILTY.

'SNAP OUT OF IT!' you say (or someone else says).

'WHAT ON EARTH DO YOU HAVE TO BE FRIGHTENED OF?'

The answer?? You're frightened of **IT**.

WHAT
IS IT?

Let's start with what **IT** ISN'T.

IT is *not* an EVIL ALIEN FORCE.

IT is *not* SPOOKS OR DEMONS.

IT is *not* DIVINE
PUNISHMENT
OR ...

...a sudden onset of insanityy...

HeeHee Hee

Hee Hee Hee

IT is *not* the work of a CRAZED GHOUL who has tampered with the water supply.

AND ...

IT does *not* come from watching too much TELEVISION!

BANG
EEEK!
SCREECH
OH!
SCREAM!
PAIN!
AARGH!
Nooo!

However, **IT** can feel VERY SCARY (this is to help your friends/family understand what you're feeling).

IT feels like you're on a CRASHING PLANE.

You feel UNSAFE in the world.

Everything that was once familiar and comforting now feels COLD, ALIEN and THREATENING.

Every minute is AGONY. You wonder
how you will get through. You feel so
TERRIFIED!

You cannot attach
your fear to
anything. There
seems to be no
REASON for **IT**.

IT is this big, awful, hideous, scary thing
that has turned your life upside down.

BUT!!
(this is for YOU now)
IT is your own PHYSICAL SENSATIONS.
IT is your own FEARFUL THOUGHTS.
IT is NOTHING MORE than this.

Believe it or not, you helped to invent your
IT all by YOURSELF!
IT is actually YOUR creation!

15

Recipe for an "IT"

(Serves none)

4 truckloads of guilt
16 cups of shoulds
4 bags of perfectionism
12 busloads of criticism (self or outside)
10 barrels of low self-esteem
20 tonnes of negative thoughts
80 kilos of exaggeration
1 football field worth of worrying
Large pinch of sense of failure
1 period of insomnia*

Combine with any of the following:

1 major life change
1 or more relationship problems
1 or more drug experiences
1 prolonged period of tension
1 set of gynaecological problems/hormonal changes
1 inability to relax
1 ridiculous workload
1 unhappy childhood
1 set of sexual problems
1 family member with Panic Syndrome or another
  anxiety disorder
1 biological predisposition

Ingredients may vary with each individual

Allow mixture to simmer for most of a lifetime.

SO ...

you have a **base** of
NEGATIVE THOUGHTS ...

to which you **add**
STRESS ...

followed by a **topping** of
PHYSICAL SENSATIONS ...

AND ...

Voila!

Your own, personal **IT**

Quite a concoction!

Let's take an even closer look at what **IT** consists of ...

EARLY CONDITIONING

Actually, you started off feeling pretty GOOD about life, yourself, and everyone else till you learned that things might not be so hunky dory after all ...

LIFE IS HARD!

FEAR *THIS,* FEAR *THAT,* FEAR EVERYTHING!

LOW SELF-ESTEEM

YOU *STUPID BOY!*

YOU HAVE TO BE CAREFUL!

... which created a BELIEF that you weren't GOOD ENOUGH as you were and that it wasn't SAFE for you to be YOU.

UNHELPFUL LIFE CHOICES

These BELIEFS informed the later CHOICES you made (including and especially the way you thought

AT LEAST HE'LL *HAVE ME!*

about yourself and what you believed you DESERVED) ...

... which led you to DOUBT yourself even more, so you pushed yourself harder to FIT IN ...

STRESSFUL THINKING STYLE

By this stage, your thinking had become pretty PUNISHING ...

CATASTROPHIC OUTLOOK

... and since you were on the lookout for TROUBLE, you started seeing it EVERYWHERE ...

ANXIOUS SET POINT

... till it became NORMAL to feel ANXIOUS!

ANTAGONISTIC COPING STYLE

Worse still, you tended to respond to STRESS with even **MORE** STRESS, till it became OVERWHELMING ...

I'M ANXIOUS THAT I'M ANXIOUS!

... and before you knew it, you'd hatched your very own pet **IT**!

HI THERE!

ITs job is to keep an eye out for POTENTIAL THREATS (real or imagined)

... and to ALERT you to them at every opportunity!

IT tells you SCARY STORIES; and he's very convincing!

And where does he get these stories?

From YOU!

If we look closely at **IT**, this is what we find ...

IT is just a pesky troublemaker who feeds you thoughts you'd be smart to ignore.

AND WHAT ARE *THOUGHTS*?

Notions that pop into your head!

WOULD I LIE TO YOU?

FLUTTER   FLUTTER

But instead, you have let him TAKE OVER!

So now, you need to REIN HIM IN!

HOUSE-
TRAINING
YOUR IT

Now that you've cooked up your **IT** and **IT** has grown legs and roams around your life making you utterly MISERABLE, you need to set down a few HOUSE RULES.

House Rule 1. ACCEPTANCE

Like him or not, your **IT**
has moved in: lock, stock
and Panic Attack. That is
the PRESENT reality.

It is difficult to accept this. You don't
WANT **IT**. You don't like **IT**.

In fact, you wouldn't wish **IT** on your
WORST ENEMY.

'No,' you think, 'there's been a mistake. **IT**
is an exotic illness.' You have a check-up,
just to
prove it.

BUT I GAVE
YOU A
CLEAN BILL
OF HEALTH!

Oh Nooo!

It's hard to live with **IT**, let alone accept
IT. You miss your old life, your old self.
You grieve for the person you THINK
you've lost forever.

It's not FAIR! **IT** is not FAIR! You want **IT**
gone, NOW! You want your life back!
How DARE **IT**
do this to you!
GO AWAY!

Guess what?
He's still THERE.

WHY?

Because when you FIGHT AGAINST
something, you actually make it BIGGER;
all of your attention is focused on the
thing you don't want!

So, stop GRIEVING and LAMENTING and
RESENTING that **IT** is here, and wishing
IT wasn't. He is. That's just the way it
is for now. What you DO about **IT** is the
more important thing.

Yes, he is BIG and UGLY and
TERRIFYING

ROAR!

But YOU designed him!

Acceptance doesn't mean that you have to
LOVE IT or even LIKE IT. In fact, right
now, you probably HATE IT — but that
doesn't change anything.

In fact, hating IT just makes you feel
worse.

Acceptance sits somewhere in between such
strong emotions. Acceptance is NEUTRAL.

You have **IT** and yes, **IT** is unpleasant, but that's how **IT** is. You HAVE **IT**, in the same way that you might HAVE a bad headache.

IT is just something you live with ... FOR NOW.

House Rule 2. BREATHING

IT is in full flight. He's having a field day. This is what you do: STOP for a few seconds and observe your breathing. It is probably SHALLOW, RAPID and high up in your chest. You may be doing an awful lot of SIGHING ...

 ... or PANTING.

You are releasing too much CARBON DIOXIDE (CO_2) and not taking in the right amount of OXYGEN. You are HYPERVENTILATING and this makes you feel weird and agitated.

NOW — without lifting your shoulders, place your hand on your abdomen and take in a big, s-l-o-w breath till your abdomen expands. Hold in the breath for FOUR counts.

Now EXHALE, with a long, SLOW breath, till your abdomen goes in. Release all the pent-up TENSION with the out-breath. Make a SOUND as you release.

KEEP GOING till you feel your breathing coming back into balance. Think ONLY of your breathing. It is the MOST IMPORTANT thing right now.

IT is CONFUSED by this. He thinks: 'Hang on, you're supposed to be SCARED and you're RELAXING! You're IGNORING me!'

Yes, you ARE ignoring **IT**. Breathing is your point of focus now. This is YOUR time. You can breathe ANYWHERE, ANY TIME that **IT** decides to bite.

For ADDED AMMUNITION, find a comfortable, quiet place to lie down. Put on some soothing music or a relaxation tape and continue with your breathing. **IT** may hang around for a while, but he HATES this New Age stuff and he HATES being ignored. He'll head off and sulk.

HRRMPH!

He's PERSISTENT, though, so you must be, too — MORE SO! Do this as often as you need to.

House Rule 3. DETACHMENT

IT may be carrying on, but that doesn't mean that you have to take any NOTICE of him. After all, he's not saying anything HELPFUL and he's not the greatest company, is he?

In your mind, cast away your trembling, snarling, biting **IT** on an island. You are safely DRIFTING BY in a small boat.

IT is raging and roaring, but you are in your boat and all you feel are DISTANT RIPPLES. **IT** is not your concern because you are just an OBSERVER, passively watching. Let **IT** roar all **IT** likes. Big deal!

Remember, **IT** is only a few TROUBLESOME THOUGHTS. He is no more sinister than that. He can't actually do you any HARM.

It may seem counter-
intuitive, but another way
to help you DETACH even
more from your **IT** is to
become INTERESTED in
him! Start to study yourself
and OBSERVE how your
IT works, without becoming emotionally
involved.

For instance, ask yourself (and keep a log
of your answers):

WHEN DOES **IT**
POP UP MOST?

WHAT AM I *THINKING*
ABOUT WHEN HE DOES?

What are the specific
physical sensations that
tell me I'm anxious?

33

Exactly WHERE in my body do
I feel them?

And what do
they actually
FEEL like? (texture,
size, colour etc.)

What do I experience in my mind and body
when I'm NOT feeling anxious?

How can I apply this knowledge to the
times when I do feel anxious?

If you can treat your **IT** like a science
project, you are less likely to take the
whole thing personally. **IT** is then just
a set of thoughts and sensations that
indicate that you're stressed or out of
balance.

House Rule 4. WAITING IT OUT

In the early stages of your life with **IT**, your distress may seem to be ENDLESS and always at an unbearable level.

IT is with you DAY after DAY, and the claw of fear in your stomach appears to be almost constant.

ALMOST ... but not totally.

In fact, even a formidable force like **IT** gets tired of pummelling you after a time. If you were to make a graph, you would find that the panic is not really constant, nor is it always at its highest pitch.

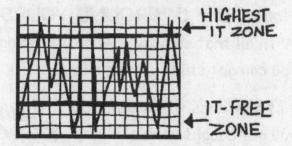

HIGHEST ← IT ZONE

IT-FREE ← ZONE

There are even some **IT**-free periods in between!

Try charting your levels of panic on a scale of 1 to 10 and see how they actually fluctuate. **IT** is not always full-on. By DEEP-BREATHING and DETACHING, it is possible to wait for the worst moments to pass.

They ALWAYS do.

Focus on that fact. Make it a chant.

Interestingly, if you were to WILL yourself to panic, you probably wouldn't. It is your FEAR of panic that makes it happen.

House Rule 5. GROUND YOURSELF
With all that endless **IT**-chatter going on, you can get stuck in your HEAD.

Not only does this mean that you get caught up in all that BLAH BLAH BLAH, but with your energy stuck in your 'attic' there's not going to be much energy left down at ground level to anchor you into nice, solid, practical earthiness!

And, boy, if ever you needed anchoring, it's now!

To ground yourself, you need to get PHYSICAL by:

DANCING
Not a waltz, by the way! You need something that thumps and pumps!

NOW *GO* FOR IT!

Boogie out the bogeyman!

SHAKIN' ALL OVER!

If you're not able to throw on a dance routine but you're feeling that **IT** has taken over, take yourself off somewhere and SHAKE **IT** off!

Again, PUSH through **IT**!

Keep going as strongly as you can till you feel your whole body TINGLING. Notice how much more 'HERE' you feel afterwards. **Alternatively**, you can:

Go for a big, stompy   or put in some
      WALK   HARD LABOUR!

Return to House Rules 1 to 5 as often as you need to.
They will help you to accept that **IT** need not overwhelm you.

      WELL DONE!

'WALKIES'
WITH IT

The first thing you are tempted to
do in your co-habitation with **IT** is ...
NOTHING! **IT** demands so much of your
time, energy and attention, you feel you
cannot take on one more thing.

IT makes you feel so overwhelmed, it's
hard to concentrate, make a decision or
perform the simplest task. He is in your

head constantly, whispering poisonous ideas. It's hard to think straight.

Eventually, you spend all your time thinking of **IT**. This feeds him, so he grows and grows till you can hardly FUNCTION any more. **IT** has pinned you down.

Perhaps your home is relatively **IT**-free. Perhaps you left him in the supermarket in Aisle 3 next to the pet food, where you first found him. Too bad you now have to do without pet food!

Or, you may have left him on a plane, whizzing around to all the places YOU would like to go!

YEAH! YEAH!

Or, **IT** may be as close as your own front gate.

IT may make you afraid of crowds or socialising or trains or dogs or bridges or music or noises or life or death or

WARS or MOVIES or POLLUTION or HAVING FUN or ...

In fact, the list can become endless. ANYTHING you associate with **IT** can make you feel PANICKY.

STOP!

Think for a minute. **IT** is YOU, remember ...

... and YOU are allowing **IT** to hold you PRISONER!

HUP, TWO THREE FOUR!

It's not the supermarket that's scary. It's just a supermarket! Your THOUGHTS about the supermarket are what is scaring you.

SCAREWAY

No matter what you are afraid of, in some way you are letting **IT** (YOU!) prevent you from enjoying YOUR life!

IT goes hand in hand with AVOIDANCE, and avoidance through PHOBIAS are **ITs** tools of trade.

The most common phobias associated with Panic Attacks are:

AGORAPHOBIA (a fear of open spaces),

CLAUSTROPHOBIA (a fear of closed spaces) and

SOCIAL PHOBIA (a fear of social situations).

A phobia develops because you link feeling afraid with being in a certain place or situation — either because you IMAGINE the worst or because of a previous scary experience. However, feeling afraid has little to do with the actual setting, but rather what you were THINKING about being in that setting.

Say you had a Panic Attack in a crowded lift. You were probably thinking:

'What if it gets stuck?'

'What if I can't get out?'

'We'll run out of air and I won't be able to breathe.'

Then, as a result of these thoughts, your breathing DOES become more shallow, your heart beats faster and you feel as though you are suffocating. Suddenly, you are DESPERATE to get out.

There is an added ingredient here, too. The lift is CROWDED.

There are strangers all around you who will see you lose CONTROL! This adds to your anxiety, so you PANIC.

From here on, you swear you will NEVER set foot in a lift again. You have developed a PHOBIA.

45

You now think you can CONTROL your fear if you compartmentalise it and AVOID exposing yourself to those frightening situations.

But avoidance actually means LOSS of control.

 Lifts are out for a start ...

 and planes, of course ...

 then trains, because they're confined too ...

 and eventually, ANY small space.

You can take charge of your **IT** by RETHINKING the situation. Acknowledge that:

- the lift DID open
- you did NOT suffocate
- most, if not all, of your fellow passengers didn't even NOTICE that you were afraid, and
- lifts are generally a very SAFE and RELIABLE form of transport.

It was your THOUGHTS that made you afraid.

Then you'd pick up the phone and call for assistance.

You may not like it but you'd deal with it, because you'd have to!

So what are you ACTUALLY afraid of?

And what is **IT**?

So all you are afraid of is ... FEELING AFRAID!

What if you lost your fear of **IT**? How would that change things?

TAKING THE BITE OUT OF IT

1. GET MOVING

When **IT** is roaring and raging, INACTIVITY will keep you focused only on how BAD you feel. This can create a VICIOUS CYCLE.

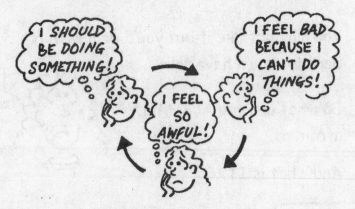

Ask yourself: What can I achieve if I DO SOMETHING?

A. I can't concentrate on **IT** and something else at the same time.

B. I could feel BETTER about myself.

C. I could feel a sense of PURPOSE.
D. I could feel I have regained some CONTROL.

SO ... Make a start. RIGHT NOW. Begin to reclaim YOUR life.

Start with small things and build on them each day.

2. MAKE A LIST

Remember, if you are going into **IT** overload, BREATHE. Tell yourself: 'This will pass.' Don't stop what you're doing! KEEP GOING! Focus on each task, not on how you're feeling. Each task is IMPORTANT.

Doing these things means that you are working to resume your life. You are taking back the reins. It helps if you bring all of your attention to whatever you're doing. This is called MINDFULNESS.

3. GET OVER YOURSELF

Feeling anxious can make you very SELF-FOCUSED. You are acutely aware of every one of your thoughts and feelings. You become very stuck in your own head. One way to shift the focus is to reach past yourself and engage with the world.

Try ringing a friend and NOT talking about your anxiety. Focus on your friend's news and what your friend is saying.

Be INTERESTED in things outside of yourself, even if only for a short time. Notice how that feels.

LISTEN to what Susie is saying. Ask QUESTIONS.

As you complete each item on your list, congratulate yourself. Each completed activity is an ACHIEVEMENT.

You did not DIE or even FAINT!

Nothing HORRIBLE happened to you!

And you know what? You may have already discovered something important about your **IT** ... that his BARK is actually far worse than his BITE!

You were still able to get things done ...

Despite feeling scared!!

Therefore ...

FEELING
SCARED
IS
NOT
IMPORTANT

Believe it or not, one day you will be
doing something and you'll realise you've
FORGOTTEN to be scared!

Eventually ...

THE
PHYSICAL
IT

One of the reasons why **IT** keeps popping up is that your mind confuses natural physical changes — especially STRESS reactions — with the first signs of an impending Panic Attack.

ABOUT STRESS

As humans, we first learned about stress when our SURVIVAL depended on it.

GRUMP GRUMP

If a sabre-toothed tiger in a bad mood happened to cross your path, your mind would flash signals to alert your body to act in your own best interests.

Your body was prepared for FLIGHT (fleeing) or FIGHT — in response to danger.

There may be no more sabre-toothed tigers, but our response to outside stressors remains the same.

Your HEART RATE increases, pumping blood into the muscles, your STOMACH tightens to move blood toward the extremities, you SWEAT to cool the skin and there is a rush of adrenalin, which causes SHAKING.

Stress reactions can even be triggered by PLEASANT sensations, such as anticipation, excitement, sexual arousal or exercise.

So — these feelings are neither good nor bad, but the way we PERCEIVE them depends on what we ASSOCIATE with them.

Stress reactions occur with:

ANXIETY

EXERTION

and

EXCITEMENT

At the start of this book, you saw the range of symptoms associated with panic.

All of these reactions occur because we perceive danger and our bodies get prepared to take on the sabre-toothed tiger — or the **IT**.

However, a Panic Attack is a FALSE ALARM. There is no tiger, but we still perceive danger.

Though there is no external threat, even a mild physical change can trigger the panic response — and the more REACTIVE you remain, the more a vicious cycle is set up.

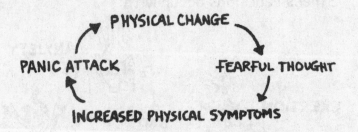

You are afraid of being afraid, and the first sign of fear is —

PHYSICAL SENSATION!

A whole range of things can set off physical changes and stress reactions.

Normally, you might not even notice them, but (remember?) you are on **IT** alert at the moment, so they can become DISTORTED or MISINTERPRETED in your mind.

Some of these triggers are:

Caffeine   Fatigue   Hunger   Alcohol

Strenuous Activity   Watching suspenseful or violent images   Hormonal Changes (Menstruation, PMS, Menopause)

Intense emotion   AND THEN...

... there are the usual daily stressors of work and relationships and deadlines and traffic jams ...

So ...

you need to learn to differentiate between EVERYDAY STRESS and PANIC ATTACKS. You need to recognise physical sensations for what they are — PHYSICAL.

Let's get a bit TECHNICAL for a moment and take a peek inside your brain to see what's going on when you're anxious.

AAARGH!

See these little horns with knobs on the end?

They're called *amygdala*.

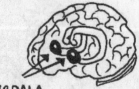

AMYGDALA

NOW   THEN

Their job is to process
STRONG EMOTION
— and this can easily
be triggered by things
in the present that
RESEMBLE things that
aroused strong emotions in the PAST!

So, for example, if you were scared
by a dog in the PAST, seeing a dog
in the present will be processed in
the same way ... with FEAR.

This little FEAR FACTORY in your head
is obediently processing your experiences
and reacting
according to
whether you
THINK there's
danger or not.

DANGER!

INCOMING!!

When you react with strong emotion, the amygdala become fired up ...

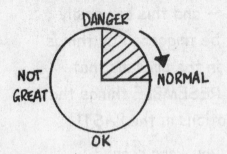

... then when the 'danger' passes, they reset to normal.

But if you keep sending fearful messages to yourself ...

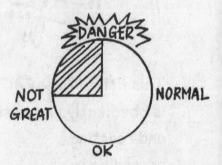

... the amygdala STAY fired up ...

... until the 'normal' setting becomes 'ANXIOUS' ...

... in which case, just about EVERYTHING sets you off!

It's important to recognise that your body and mind are simply being OBEDIENT. They're just processing the information they're receiving from YOU.

I FEEL REVVED UP ALL THE TIME!

Your **IT** is simply telling you that your system is OUT OF BALANCE.

Say to yourself ...

THIS IS JUST MY BODY'S RESPONSE TO MY *THOUGHTS!* THERE IS NO ACTUAL *DANGER!*

Remove fearful thoughts and things start to calm down again; the amygdala can reset, your whole system can settle and you'll feel LESS ANXIOUS.

So let's get working on that THINKING right now!

65

THE
THINKING
IT OWNER

CHECKLIST FOR AN IT OWNER

Not everyone qualifies to own an **IT**. You need to be a special kind of thinker. **Try this checklist:**

- ❑ I worry a lot over things that might not happen.
- ❑ I tend to exaggerate.
- ❑ I expect to be able to deal with ANYTHING.
- ❑ I strive for perfection but fail to achieve it.
- ❑ I feel that, when compared to others, I am lacking.
- ❑ I expect to be liked by and to like everyone.
- ❑ I often find it difficult to handle my emotions.
- ❑ I am not happy with my appearance most of the time.
- ❑ I tend to push myself too hard.
- ❑ I do not 'suffer fools gladly'.
- ❑ I tend not to make time to relax.
- ❑ I find that my emotions spill over easily.

or

❑ I have difficulty in showing my
  emotions.

❑ I spend a lot of time thinking about old
  hurts, injustices and regrets.

❑ I worry about what people think of me.

❑ I feel uneasy/scared if I cannot
  control a situation.

❑ I tend to criticise others and myself.

❑ I often find myself thinking 'I should'
  or 'I wish' or 'what if'.

❑ I have trouble 'letting go' of a situation.

❑ I feel the need to be right.

IT owners are great THINKERS. They
do lots of it, and lots of that thinking is
NEGATIVE, otherwise they wouldn't own
an **IT**!

Remember the recipe? Ingredients like
CRITICISM, GUILT, WORRY ... that's
your **IT**.

So it's time to see **IT** for what he really
is ...

A NAG

IT is that voice in your head, telling you over and over that you BLEW THIS, or MESSED UP that, or that you're NOT GOOD ENOUGH, or that you're FOOLISH — too this, too that; that it's ALWAYS this or NEVER that; that you SHOULD be better, but you CAN'T do anything — you're HOPELESS, INCOMPETENT, UGLY, LAZY, DIFFICULT, BAD, WEAK, PATHETIC ... on and on and on, nag, nag, nag, day in, day out.

69

He's even started to brag about himself
lately, hasn't he?
He says ...

I can make
you panic
WHENEVER
I want!

You're stuck
with me
FOREVER!

I'm
BIGGER
than you
are!

You're
HOPELESS!
I'm in
CONTROL!

IT has a whole LIST of thought patterns
to use on you and bring you down ...

Here are the main ones ...

1. EITHER/OR

You see one bad situation as the PERMANENT situation. Either you're dazzling this time, or you never were!

2. BLAME ME

EVERYTHING is YOUR fault and YOUR responsibility: the weather, the behaviour of your guests, your company's bankruptcy, your spouse's cooking.

If there's a problem — you caused it!

3. ONE GOOF=TOTAL GOOF!

One mistake and that's it. You'll NEVER be any good; you ALWAYS mess up! NO-ONE makes as many mistakes as you!

4. BAD TAGS

A whole dictionary of clichés and put-downs that bundles everyone into little sealed, tagged boxes – used widely by *fascists*, *idiots* and *wimps* (see??).

5. SELECTIVE MEMORY

Whoops! what colour are those glasses? certainly not rose! Did you tell your friend about the great cruise, the friendly service, the beautiful scenery and the

night you danced on the tables with
25 new friends?

Somehow, you forgot all that.

6. ME, ME, ME

Uh oh. The whole universe centres around
YOU. You are being judged and observed
for your faults all the time.

You enter a room. Either everyone
is STARING at you or everyone is
IGNORING you. (P.S. They're not!)

7. CLAIRVOYANCE

Oh, the pitfalls of amateur telepathy! And you just know that facial flicker on the other person means bad news for you! How could they be thinking anything good about you?

8. THE SKY IS FALLING!

Chicken Little was probably the first to introduce total freak-out into folklore, but **IT**-owners make it an art form. Your mind leaps from one (surmountable) problem through a whole series of spin-offs that have you arriving at total annihilation!

And one of **IT**s all-time favourites is:

What if I'm late?

What if I make a fool of myself?

What if I faint?

What if I die?

What if the plane crashes/

the bridge collapses/

the lift gets stuck/

the world blows up?

By far the best antidote to the 'What if?' question is to ANSWER it!

Ask yourself: What's the worst thing that **IT** could do to me?

SEE?

Worry, worry, worry. We use worry as if it is some kind of insurance that will prevent disaster!

> IF I JUST *WORRY* ABOUT THIS ENOUGH, IT MIGHT NOT *HAPPEN!*

And worrying about ANXIETY just keeps you focused on **IT**. So why are you surprised when he shows up, as you expected he would?

BOO!!

> I HOPE I DON'T GET ANXIOUS!

> WHERE DID *YOU* COME FROM?!

Be aware of what you're asking for! Are you asking for TROUBLE?

Oh and here's a tip ... wait for something to actually HAPPEN before you REACT to it!

And when you can turn 'What if?' into 'So what?', you'll know you're really getting somewhere!

This chapter has explored just a sample of those **IT** whispers that have pulled you down, day after day, year after year.

No wonder you're feeling bad!

What a bore! What a drag! What a party pooper!

What a bundle of dead weight to heave around! Where does he get this stuff from, anyway?

Notice how there are no grey areas in **IT** statements.
They are inflexible absolutes:
EVERYTHING, ALWAYS, EVERYBODY, NO-ONE, NEVER, EVER, TOTALLY, COMPLETELY.

Then there are his weapon words:

HAVE TO, GOT TO, MUST, OUGHT TO, SUPPOSED TO, SHOULD.

How much do you live your life to an idea of 'should' or 'must'?

Who says you should?

Who says you must?

Who says you have to?

Who's making the rules on how you live your life?

And why do you think this is a royal decree?

Oh yes, **IT** is so sure. **IT** just knows.

IT is clearly an expert on what's best for you!

Isn't it time you asked yourself:

Not exactly a reliable source, is **IT** really?

Has it ever occurred to you that **IT** never has anything GOOD to say???

The only thing that **IT** is an expert at is scaring the hell out of you!

Why do you take what he says so SERIOUSLY?

FACING IT

If someone subjected your best friend to the kind of punishment that **IT** doles out to you, surely you would intervene.

You would DEFEND them.

You would seek out further evidence before jumping to CONCLUSIONS.

You would refuse to indulge in UGLY GOSSIP about them.

You would appreciate their INDIVIDUALITY ...

... and accept that, at times, they have views that do not fit OTHERS' IDEALS.

DON'T BE SILLY; IT'S JUST AN OLD MING!

You would FORGIVE them for being HUMAN ...

You would offer SUPPORT ...

HELP them find solutions to their problems ...

and you would not expect the IMPOSSIBLE from them.

In other words ...

YOU'RE A GOOD FRIEND!

That is, to everyone except YOURSELF.

Boy, are you HARD on yourself!

It's time to change the way you TALK TO and THINK ABOUT YOURSELF!

83

Your thoughts actually create most of what you experience. If your thoughts are NEGATIVE and ANXIOUS, that's what you EXPECT and that's what you'll find.

But your thoughts CAN be changed, simply because you learned to think that way in the first place!

It's a matter of re-educating yourself to consistently think in a way that soothes rather than scares you.

And, like any new skill, this takes PRACTICE.

STEPS TOWARDS CHANGING YOUR THINKING

Let's do a bit of talking back to **IT**! He's held the floor for ages now, UNCHALLENGED. Now it's your turn. Let's start with Panic Attacks.

Step 1. CHECK THE STORY

Ask yourself if the negative statement is actually TRUE. Could you be exaggerating or distorting?

Step 2. DEMAND EVIDENCE

What is the idea based on? What are the FACTS?

Step 3. DEAL WITH THE 'WHAT IFs'

Ask yourself: Realistically, what is the WORST that could happen?

Step 4. GIVE YOURSELF A BREAK

Do things HAVE to go a particular way? There are always other options. Give yourself an 'out' and you'll be more likely to relax.

Step 5. SCRAP THOSE ABSOLUTES

Get this: you can do whatever you like! You can actually choose to do what's best for YOU alone!

Step 6. INDULGE THE GOOD TIMES

If it happens that you catch yourself feeling GOOD, indulge yourself. Give yourself permission. Don't self-sabotage.

GO ON — BE A FRIEND — TO YOURSELF.

BUT BEING *POSITIVE* SEEMS *PHONY!* IT'S NOT *REALISTIC!* ALL THAT *HAPPY, HAPPY* STUFF— *YUK!*

If you want to be REALISTIC, consider this: you've told yourself '**YUK**', and '*YUK*' is the REALITY you've got.

Interesting, yes?

If you LIKE your reality the way it is, keep telling yourself things like:

LIFE SUCKS!

I CAN'T DO ANYTHING RIGHT!

EVERYTHING IS RUINED!

That's what you'll GET.

No, what you're presenting is BIASED REPORTING. These are not facts. This is simply your OPINION of your current situation as seen on one particular day. It could all look completely different tomorrow!

Look, if you can't quite get to being Pollyanna, at least be a bit more careful about what you THINK and SAY — and notice the difference this makes to how you FEEL.

THINKING, NOT PANICKING

You will need to do a bit of work on your thinking even when **IT** is off dozing somewhere.

As we saw earlier in this section, there are a lot of nasty whispers in your head that have helped to create your **IT** in the first place.

TRY THESE TACTICS ...

Ask: 'Do I really have enough EVIDENCE to reach a conclusion?'

Leave the PREDICTIONS to the soothsayers!

WHAT A WEIRDO!!

Hey! No NAME-CALLING, OK?

If something doesn't go to plan ... look for the BEST option! (Or at least stop seeking out the WORST one!)

There ARE alternatives.

REMEMBER: No-one and nothing can MAKE you feel a certain way. YOU govern your feelings and you have a CHOICE in how you respond.

We all have good days ... and not-so-good days.

HOWEVER — it's all just part of the
RICH TAPESTRY OF LIFE!

(P.S. Learn to love clichés.)

Feeling **LOUSY?**

Avoid COMPARING yourself to others.

Maybe it's not cancer or a brain tumour or something terminal after all! Maybe you're just TIRED or STRESSED.

... some things just can't be helped.

Does it really MATTER what most people think of you?

This may come as a SHOCK ... but you are NOT the centre of the universe!

Be realistic about getting things done. Find a BALANCE. Pace yourself.

After all ... is the deadline really a life or death line?

Acknowledge your ACHIEVEMENTS!

EVERYBODY?

Does EVERYBODY
have to like you?
it's a good idea not

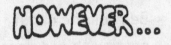

to jump to conclusions!

AND LASTLY ... (but not least!) you are
not **SUPER PERSON**.

Have you noticed something?

IT is not QUITE as powerful as he was.

Even if you've only just begun, even if you notice only the slightest shift, you have already made PROGRESS. You have started to reclaim your life.

BE PATIENT with yourself. You are learning SKILLS you may not have used before. It takes TIME to adjust. It takes time to HEAL.

You will need to be committed to progress. **IT** hates you being OPTIMISTIC. He thrives when you feed him your DOOM, GLOOM and HOPELESSNESS.

He also loves OVER-REACTIONS and DISTORTIONS. Stop feeding him these, and

HERE'S A
MIRROR

TAKE A
LOOK

You are actually a NICE, NORMAL human being who has gotten into your own unique kind of muddle.

What person on Earth hasn't, at some time or other?

You DESERVE to be as happy as everyone else!

You're doing the best you can for now and as you gain confidence, you'll do even BETTER!

Memorise this ➡️

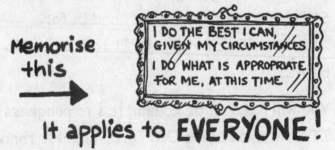

> I DO THE BEST I CAN, GIVEN MY CIRCUMSTANCES
> I DO WHAT IS APPROPRIATE FOR ME, AT THIS TIME //

It applies to EVERYONE!

TRY THIS: Observe the differences between others and yourself without JUDGEMENT for just one day.

No labels, no categories, no put-downs, no name-calling. It's very liberating to do this. Why? Because the pressure's off.

· You no longer need to COMPETE with

or IMPRESS those you believe are superior.

- You no longer have to COMPARE yourself to others.
- You no longer have to feel frustrated or angry with others, because now you are IMPARTIAL.
- You no longer need to feel that some people are out of bounds because they are BETTER or WORSE than you.

You don't have to PROVE your worth.

You just need to EMBRACE it.

Take yourself AS YOU ARE.

Take others AS THEY ARE.

If you can do this exercise for one day, then why not try it all the time? It's POWERFUL. It's a RELIEF.

So as a final stunning tactic ... Give everybody (including yourself) a HOLIDAY!

NON-IT
OWNERS

This is about the people you encounter;
the people you share the world with,
be they family, friends, colleagues or
strangers.

They may say ...

These responses could leave you feeling
WORSE. You could feel MISUNDERSTOOD
or that your pain has been TRIVIALISED;
or you might feel GUILTY for feeling bad
for no (apparent) reason.

Then again — there will be people who say ...

All these people are reacting in ways that are APPROPRIATE TO THEM (remember?) and in response to several factors:

- Their own experience
- Their own personality
- Their own level of understanding
- Their own ability to empathise
- Their own ability to express their feelings
- Their own problems
- Their own ability to cope
- Their own set of beliefs.

There will be some people who will be more RECEPTIVE than others. Don't be afraid to ask for help, but don't beat yourself up if some people don't 'GET **IT**'. Not everyone can.

It's also important to remember that **IT** may be impacting on those closest to you almost as much as it is on YOU.

This is NOT an excuse for a GUILT TRIP, so DON'T GO THERE! Rather, this is just asking you to make allowances for people behaving a bit unusually, too, instead of getting FREAKED OUT by this.

They, too, may be TIRED ...

... or FRUSTRATED

Hi dear, I'm home!

... or they may feel HELPLESS

There goes Dad again!

... or even ANGRY.

This doesn't mean they love you less. Often they simply do not know what to DO.

HERE'S WHAT THEY CAN DO

(show them this)

1. LISTEN

Panicking People need to let it out. OFTEN.
Panicking People need to talk it through.
OFTEN.

2. ENCOURAGE

Recognising that the Panicking Person is
trying will spur them on. Encourage them
to keep going, but never bully them or
become impatient. They are doing their
best. They need your SUPPORT.

3. BE THE VOICE OF REASON

If the Panicking Person is feeling chaotic,
step in and guide them back to a point of
FOCUS. Encourage them to STEP BACK
and THINK IT THROUGH rather than let

their feelings run away with them. Reason it out together.

4. UNDERSTAND that this is very real to the Panicking Person. There may be very severe physical symptoms.

5. AVOID SURPRISES
The Panicking Person needs to pace him/herself. They may need to plan ahead, so they can deal with each new situation.

6. ACKNOWLEDGE EACH ACHIEVEMENT

I'm proud of you!

However insignificant it may seem to you, to the Panicking Person completing a new task may have meant climbing a mountain. Remind them, too, of their PROGRESS. They may forget at times.

7. TRY TO BE PATIENT

1-2-3-

This is hard, but getting angry or showing frustration will only make the Panicking Person feel GUILTY. It takes time and effort to change — and remember, you are WELL; you have more reserves to call on.

8. BECOME INFORMED

It is a great help if you know about the strategies that will help the person through to recovery. You can then work with them to achieve their goal and return BOTH of your lives to normal.

You, the Panicking Person, can also help your family and friends by telling them what YOU need them to do if you're panicking.

However, while we're here, let's take another look at **IT** and the part he plays in all this.

You may be surprised to know that **IT** has actually been trying to PROTECT you by keeping alert for DANGER.

INCOMING!

And what's the BIGGEST POTENTIAL THREAT to you as far as **IT** is concerned?

OTHER PEOPLE!

Again, this goes back to our caveman days.

If you weren't accepted by the tribe, your life would be in peril.

Being REJECTED is still one of our greatest fears.

OUT!

So **IT** is now on the lookout for ways that you don't FIT IN and alerts you of these things, in case you're left out in the cold.

So much of your anxiety rests on your self-worth being governed by OTHERS' OPINIONS that I've written a whole book about the subject (*I Love Me*). But for now, here's all you need to know:

- People will behave exactly as they want to. Wanting them to behave differently to make YOU feel better is futile.
- Your job is to attend to your own needs, REGARDLESS of what anyone else is doing.

- Your wellbeing is entirely YOUR business and YOUR responsibility. No-one else's.
- People can only help you to help YOURSELF. Stop looking for 'rescue'.
- No-one knows what's best for you as well as you do!
- Having anxiety doesn't mean you're FLAWED — it just means you've become SENSITISED.

OWNING

YOUR IT

You have probably asked the following questions many times:

Question 1. WHY ME??

WHY ME??

Why is this awful, terrible, hideous thing happening to ME?

There are basic problems with this line of thinking. The very question 'Why me?' suggests that **IT** comes from the outside, as if you have been selected in a giant cosmic lottery and your **IT** has been ALLOTTED to you.

NUMBER 1 REPORT TO 16 SUNNYSIDE DRIVE, NUMBER 2...

This concept can work against you in several ways.

By believing that **IT** has been IMPOSED on you, you give **IT** control. You become a VICTIM, waiting to be rescued.

In this situation, **IT** can take on many guises.

IT can be other people who make you feel uneasy.

IT can be places that make you feel scared.

Or **IT** can appear
in situations that
make you feel
uncomfortable.

Did you spot the FLAW in the above
statements?

Nothing can MAKE you feel a certain way.

No-one can MAKE you feel a certain way.

Your feelings belong to YOU.

It's the same with **IT**. When you see **IT** as
something that HAPPENS to you, outside
of your control, you give **IT** ABSOLUTE
POWER over your life.

Question 2. WHAT HAVE I DONE TO DESERVE THIS?

This suggests that you are being PUNISHED. But by WHOM? For WHAT?

You are not being punished.
You are not BAD. You are not WRONG.
Your thinking has become a bit wonky,
that's all.

Let's observe your thinking in everyday situations:

Say you've had a BAD DAY (everybody has them!) —

1. You oversleep and are late for work ...

Do you say:

IF THE HOURS WERE MORE FLEXIBLE I WOULDN'T BE LATE!

OR

I'M SORRY I'M LATE BUT I'LL MAKE UP THE TIME

2. You lose an important file. Do you say:

3. Your car breaks down. Do you say:

In each of these examples, you have the choice to either externalise the situation and apportion BLAME (it's the clock's, your boss's, someone's fault), or to OWN your part in the situation and take steps to RECTIFY it.

The same goes for **IT**.

Fighting **IT**, blaming **IT**, wringing your hands about **IT** and worrying about **IT** only feeds POWER to **IT** and therefore, away from you!

And as long as you see yourself as a helpless VICTIM, you remain powerless; not only with regard to **IT** but in LIFE, too.

Take back your power!

OWN the ways that you keep your **IT** alive. From now on, take RESPONSIBILITY for the THOUGHTS and WORDS you choose to entertain.

No-one else can change your thinking for you. Fixing **IT** is YOUR job ...

... and you're the boss of what comes next!

Question 3. BUT HOW DID I GET IT IN THE FIRST PLACE?

It's natural to want to find a CAUSE; something to pin these awful feelings on. But we are complex beings and the causes may  also be complex, numerous and sometimes HIDDEN.

Ask yourself: if you knew right now that the reason you have **IT** is that you nearly drowned as a child (for instance), would that make **IT** totally DISAPPEAR?

Probably not, because you have developed a PATTERN OF THINKING  about your anxiety that needs to be adjusted in the HERE and NOW.

Think of all the ENERGY and ATTENTION you are giving to **IT**, for instance.

When you are anxious, you perceive every experience, sensation, encounter and situation only in terms of how they impact on your anxiety levels.

Focusing on a cause may only ADD to your anxiety because, again, you are making ANXIETY the centre of your attention.

Get on with getting better. There will be time to delve into the whys and wherefores later if you wish, and you will then be able to follow your search from a position of STRENGTH.

Dealing with your situation, and staying in the HERE and NOW helps to anchor you.

HOWEVER, it's also good to learn from the past in order to make IMPROVEMENTS in the future, so if you find delving in that context helpful, go for it!

The bottom line is: if it helps, do it. If it doesn't, don't!

BEFRIENDING
YOUR **IT**

This may surprise you, but we're not trying to get rid of **IT**! He's actually not a bad guy, he's just MISUNDERSTOOD!

BUT **IT** IS SO ALL-CONSUMING! I'M NOT *MYSELF* WHEN I HAVE IT!

But **IT** is an aspect of YOU! Getting rid of **IT** would mean getting rid of YOU!

WELL JUST WHAT ASPECT OF ME IS **IT**?

Well, here's a question — how OLD do you feel when you're ANXIOUS?

ABOUT 6, I GUESS!

Then that's your **IT** — just a SCARED KID acting out!

If you think of your **IT** as just a kid running amok, then you can clearly see what DOESN'T work:

- Trying to reason with **IT**
- Arguing with **IT**
- Fighting back
- Trying to block **IT** out.

In much the same way as you would an unruly child:

- Don't feed into the hysteria
- Shift the focus away from **IT**
- Don't take what **IT** says too seriously or personally
- See **IT** for what **IT** really is (troublesome thoughts), instead of what **IT** seems to be (reality)
- Accept **IT**s unruly nature
- Be calm and he'll calm down too
- Be the grown-up! Who's in charge?

It's actually possible to make **IT** your ALLY instead of your enemy.

YOU'RE *KIDDING!* HOW CAN I DO *THAT?*

Change your relationship with him!

Try some TEAMWORK!

Notice when your **IT** pops up most:

In other words ... when you're being MEAN to yourself!

This is when **IT** can be very helpful. He can alert you to the things that need your ATTENTION.

IT can tell you when you're:
- overdoing things
- repressing feelings
- being judgemental
- comparing yourself to others
- worrying about what others think
- being hard on yourself
- avoiding a tough decision
- not asserting yourself

- suppressing anger
- and especially when you're slipping back into 'stinky thinking'!

Give your **IT** a purpose. LISTEN to what he has to tell you!

THESE are the things that are really making you anxious. **IT** has just been REPORTING on them!

IT simply tells you when to change your tune! He's your in-built NEGATIVITY MONITOR.

RECRUITING
AN IT
OBEDIENCE
INSTRUCTOR

Your particular **IT** may still be a bit too much of a handful to take on all by yourself at first. He may be keeping you up at all hours, demanding your attention.

His favourite trick is to stand on your chest so that you can't breathe properly, or to make your heart race, or to confuse you into thinking that you're stuck with him forever! You're probably EXHAUSTED.

So — call in the troops!

A good counsellor will help you house-train your **IT**, by guiding you through the steps towards recovery and helping you to recognise areas of stress in your life and the way you deal with them.

He/she will also assist you in finding your OWN solutions to problems that might be causing conflict or unhappiness in your life, and he/she will help you modify the patterns of thinking or behaviour that may be holding you back.

A good counsellor will serve as a CONFIDANTE and FRIEND, so choose someone with whom you feel very comfortable.

Most importantly, you will have someone to talk to who understands how you feel, and who will be able to actively assist you in returning to your normal life.

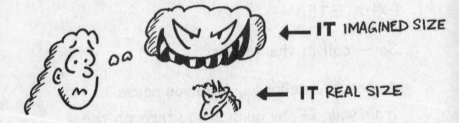

← **IT** IMAGINED SIZE

← **IT** REAL SIZE

If your symptoms are particularly severe or debilitating, your therapist may suggest DRUGS in the early stages of your **IT**

128

encounter. Drugs can be a way for you to get some REST and thereby help you regain STRENGTH and some emotional 'space' to get **IT** into PERSPECTIVE.

If you have any concerns about medication, ensure that you discuss these thoroughly with your therapist and/or GP.

Remember: Ultimately, it's YOUR choice, so be INFORMED.

Note: Drugs are designed to deal with the changes in your BRAIN CHEMISTRY. While drugs may give you some RELIEF, do not mistake them for a CURE.

You will still need to explore the underlying FACTORS that caused you to become anxious in the first place.

For example: if you suffer from MIGRAINES, you may take medication to give you PAIN RELIEF ...

... but then to lessen the possibility
of FURTHER attacks, you will need to
eliminate the things that TRIGGER
headaches, such as certain

FOODS

LIFESTYLE
FACTORS

and STRESSES.

You will need to attend to your ANXIETY
TRIGGERS in the same way, and
counselling can help you to identify and
resolve the underlying issues behind your
anxiety.

IT'S BACK!

SETBACKS

Just when you thought it was safe ...

SURPRISE!

Oh not again! It's the return of **IT**! Well, he's persistent. After all, he's had years of practice!

O.K. THINK about it!!

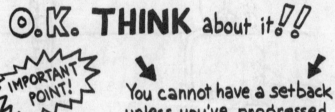

IMPORTANT POINT!

You cannot have a setback unless you've <u>progressed</u> in the first place!

So — having setbacks means you're getting better!

You are not at BASE 1 because you've already been there, done that! The only way from here is FORWARD.

BUT IT FEELS LIKE I HAVE TO START *ALL OVER AGAIN!*

But this time, you know what to DO! Before, you didn't. Now you're just figuring out what WORKS and what doesn't.

What happens when you really APPLY what you have learned in this book?

WELL, I DO FEEL LESS *ANXIOUS* —THAT'S *TRUE!*

In other words, you feel BETTER?

A LITTLE— UNTIL *IT* COMES *BACK,* THAT IS!

Surely a LITTLE is better than NOT AT ALL!

If you keep building on that, with PRACTICE, you'll become an EXPERT!

So if thinking less anxiously makes you feel BETTER, why aren't you doing so ALL THE TIME?

IT'S *HARD* TO CHANGE MY *THINKING!*

Anxiety's HARDER, isn't it?

Besides, 'It's hard' is a BELIEF — and not a helpful one. What if you thought of this work as interesting, important or liberating instead?

Because that's exactly what it is.

He went away before, didn't he? Just handle him the same way as you did last time.

BUT WHEN **IT** REAPPEARS I WORRY THAT HE'LL *STAY!*

Eventually, you'll get better at it, (or **IT**)
and you'll move on quicker.

What if you just ACCEPT that **IT** will pop up
now and then ... till **IT** doesn't anymore?

Here's the bottom line: you feel anxious and
you want to feel less anxious. If you want to
feel less anxious, this is the work involved.

It will take as long as it takes. Just keep
going. Isn't your WELLBEING worth the
effort?

You're STRONGER now, because you're
better INFORMED. You know what to do.

HERE ARE SOME REMINDERS:

Thousands of people have
overcome panic. You can too.

Each time you feel anxious,
use CORRECT BREATHING ...

GIVE
IT
(and yourself)
TIME ... It will pass

You are only afraid of FEAR! (which is just some troublesome thoughts)

AND ... Hop in your boat and FLOAT past the worst of **IT**.

1. Question the truth of the thoughts.
2. Demand evidence.
3. Reason it out.
4. Supply a better option.

TUNE INTO YOUR THINKING →

Are you back to old habits?

Remember— feeling scared is not IMPORTANT! Keep doing things! Keep busy!

KATHUMP! KATHUMP!!

Are you confusing FEAR with PHYSICAL SENSATIONS?

Make friends with yourself.

Acknowledge all that you've achieved!

SETBACKS are just part of the journey towards full recovery. It is not a matter of being in full panic mode one day, then not the next; it's more like an EVOLUTION. You evolved into anxiety; now you need to evolve out of it.

Let's face it, you've developed a HABIT of feeling BAD. Now you need to make a habit of helping yourself feel BETTER, till it becomes natural to do so!

Recovery is a GRADUAL building process. This is because you need to relearn (or learn for the first time) a set of SKILLS, and one is how to desensitise yourself to situations, sensations and locations that you would normally associate with being afraid.

This work requires PRACTICE and exposure, till finally you are able to separate places, feelings and ideas from the panic you feel.

You now have a whole kitbag of strategies to help you build RECOVERY.

All you need to do is make sure you USE them! AGAIN and AGAIN if need be — how else do you become skillful?

Above all, don't resent it (or **IT**). This is the work involved in healing your LIFE, and the benefits of this work go well beyond overcoming anxiety.

And it was **IT** who brought you here.

But with every step, you remove yourself
FURTHER and FURTHER from those first
difficult days with **IT**.

Focus on your PROGRESS and not
on your PAIN. Be committed to your
WHOLENESS, not your MISERY.

Assess what you are doing right now.
Are you working TOO HARD? Can you
pace things more gently? Is something
bothering you that you need to CHANGE?
Have you encountered a situation you find
difficult to handle? Can you ask for HELP?

Can you be NICER to yourself?

This is TEMPORARY. This will PASS.

You WILL be all right!

A FINAL WORD

It's hard to see right now, but you have been presented with an opportunity ...

TO FEEL BETTER ABOUT YOURSELF
TO FEEL BETTER ABOUT OTHERS
TO FEEL BETTER ABOUT LIFE

You are learning how to be KINDER to yourself.

You are learning how OLD HABITS OF THINKING have held you back.

You are learning PATIENCE, ACCEPTANCE and TOLERANCE.

AND ... you are learning to focus on the things that will help you PROGRESS, not just now, but throughout your ENTIRE LIFE!

Maybe meeting **IT** was not such a BAD thing, after all!

If you change the way you feel about YOURSELF, then you may change the way you see **IT**.

After all, **IT** is YOU and YOU are **IT**.

You might never find him COMPLETELY lovable ...

... but at least you can make PEACE.

AFTER ALL...

I know a **SURVIVOR** when I see one!

TURN THE PAGE
FOR MORE BEV AISBETT
BOOKS

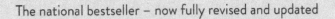

The national bestseller – now fully revised and updated

TAMING THE BLACK DOG

OVER
200,000
COPIES
SOLD

A GUIDE TO OVERCOMING
DEPRESSION
BEV AISBETT

Don't want to get out of bed in the morning? Feeling as though the light is fading at the end of the tunnel? If so, you could be suffering from depression, or as Winston Churchill used to call it, 'the black dog'.

Taming the Black Dog, which was first published in 2000, is Bev Aisbett's bestselling, simple and easy-to-follow guide to overcoming depression. It has sold over 220,000 copies and helped thousands of people manage their depression.

Now expanded and updated, this fully revised edition of *Taming the Black Dog* features Bev Aisbett's unique blend of information, humour and clear practical advice. It is an invaluable guide and source of information for chronic sufferers of depression as well as anyone who's ever had a fit of the 'blues'. More than 1 in 5 people will suffer some form of depression at some point in their lives, so *Taming the Black Dog* is a more importance resource than ever before.

30 DAYS 30 WAYS

TO OVERCOME ANXIETY

> "Bev Aisbett is a gift. Her simple, easy-to-follow advice about anxiety is revelatory. Bev has helped my family and several friends through the most difficult of times. She can help you, too."
>
> **Cameron Daddo**

BEV AISBETT

National bestselling author of *Living with IT*

From Australia's bestselling anxiety expert, Bev Aisbett, comes a proven and practical workbook to help people manage their anxiety, with simple daily strategies for work and for home.

Based on many of the exercises Bev has been teaching and writing about for the past twenty years, the book provides clear, simple daily building blocks to help people manage their anxiety and assist them in their recovery. Designed to be carried in handbags or backpacks as a daily companion, this is a highly approachable, concise, practical, simple and, above all, proven method of overcoming anxiety.